The Getaway Guy

50 MORE Day Trip Getaways with Mike O'Brian

Written by Mike O'Brian

www.thegetawayguy.com

Published by

Earthquake Company
www.earthquakeco.com
Rochester, NY
© Copyright 2013

ISBN 978-0-615-78599-8

Printed in the United States of America
Design by Chad Taggart
Edited by Brandon Taggart

Thank you for purchasing The Getaway Guy: Volume 2! This book was created to help you enjoy the many wonderful destinations our area has to offer. Please visit our website for exclusive travel deals, tips and news. www.thegetawayguy.com

Special thanks to:
Geneva on the Lake
Greek Peak Mountain Resort
Mercury Print Productions
Time Warner Cable

To all the fans who relentlessly demanded
a second travel book...this one's for you!

Mike O'Brian...The Getaway Guy!

Born in Corning, New York, Mike O'Brian began his broadcasting career in 1971 at Rochester radio station WSAY. Stations like WBBF and WVOR followed, with a brief time in Tampa, Florida at WQXM radio. Mike's on-air experience in radio prepared him for his career in television. He joined Time Warner Cable News in 1995 and is known for his TV travels around the state as The Getaway Guy.

"Travel has always been my passion and now I can bring all of my favorite getaways to viewers."

In addition to New York State getaways, Mike loves traveling the back roads of the New England Coast, and tries to make time each winter to visit the Caribbean. The American southwest is also a favorite destination of his. In between getaways, Mike devotes time to local and regional voice-over work, something he has enjoyed doing for many years.

There's not a lot of spare time left in a day, but when there is, Mike enjoys working in his back yard, entertaining friends and working off some occasional stress at the gym. Most of the time you'll find Mike behind the wheel, on another road trip, ready to enjoy his greatest passion.

"I get great satisfaction when people tell me how much they really enjoyed traveling to one of my recent Getaways!"

Handicap Accessible

 Great for the entire family

 Don't forget the camera

 A nice Getaway for couples

 For those who like a little adventure

 Open year round

 You might get wet

 Dining available

 Great for animal lovers

 Overnight accommodations

 Historical value

Attention!

This book uses QR Codes (quick response) to help you easily connect to maps on your GPS enabled smartphone. It only takes a few simple steps:

1. Visit the app store on your smartphone
2. Search 'QR code reader'
3. Download one of the free readers and open it up
4. Scan the QR code!

Here, try one. This one brings you to The Getaway Guy's website!

Table of Contents

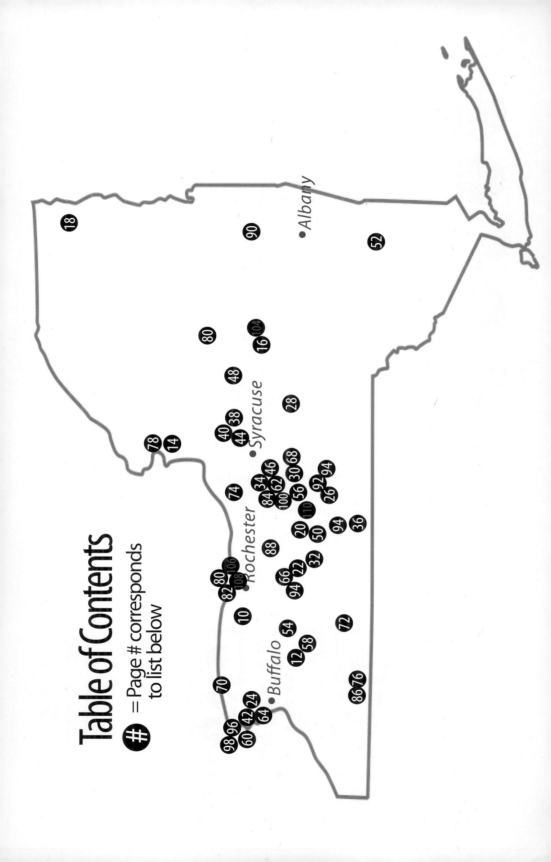

= Page # corresponds
to list below

 = Page # corresponds to map above

Simply New York

4364 Culver Road
Rochester, NY 14622
(585) 413-0895
www.simplynystore.com

Like the Travel Book... this store is all about New York State! From dinnerware to outerwear, high quality products manufactured right here in our state! Open daily! Check website for hours.

When I travel in the Seabreeze area, I always stop in because I know I'll find something I like. I love local! - The Getaway Guy

Redwood Restaurant

6 Cohocton Street
Naples, NY 14512
(585) 374-6360

If you find yourself hungry for breakfast in Naples, NY, grab a seat at the coffee shop counter! Good eggs, bacon and home fries! Your coffee cup won't go empty! Open Moday through Saturday from 6am and Sunday from 7am.

This is where the locals go! And it's where I go for breakfast when I'm in town!
- The Getaway Guy

Recommended!

Quality Wine Tours

(585) 455-8294
Toll Free 877-424-7004
www.qualitywinetours.com

When touring the wineries in the Finger Lakes, let Quality Wine Tours be your designated driver! Service 7 days a week to Keuka, Cayuga, Seneca and Canandaigua Lakes! A safe, responsible and fun way to see the area.

I can't think of a better way to tour the Finger Lakes! The service is perfect! — The Getaway Guy

The Garden Factory

2126 Buffalo Road
Rochester, NY 14624
(585) 247-6236
www.gardenfactoryny.com

Pretty much anytime of year, this popular garden store in Gates, NY literally becomes a seasonal local Getaway, with big family-oriented events! From their endless fall fun in autumn, to over-the-top holiday events in December, this is more than a great garden center! It's a destination! Open every day from 8am!

I love the model train display set up for the holidays! One of the biggest around, it is an important part of what makes holidays so special for kids and families!

— The Getaway Guy

Adams Basin Inn

Adams Basin, NY

For a quiet and peaceful B&B Getaway with a touch of history and country elegance, consider the Adams Basin Inn Bed & Breakfast in Adams Basin, N.Y.

An easy 13-mile ride out of Rochester, this B&B is located right on the Erie Canal which makes it perfect for scenic walks and bike rides on the canal path. The inn has been a home to many travelers since the 1800's! Boasting the only 'intact' tavern on the Erie Canal may have a lot to do with the inn being on the National and State Registry of Historic Homes!

There are four very comfy and cozy guest rooms. I was drawn to the Michael Ryan Room because of its private outdoor balcony overlooking the canal! All rates include a full gourmet breakfast and the food is so good, Pat has written her own cookbook! Innkeepers Pat & David Haines will see to your every need!

Adams Basin Inn

425 Washington Street
Adams Basin, NY 14410

**Scan for map.
Learn how on page 5.**

Info:

(585) 352-3999
www.adamsbasininn.com
Open year round
$115-$145 per night / double occupancy with breakfast included

Travel Tip:

How romantic! The Inn now has hot air balloon flights arranged
through Liberty Balloon Company!
www.libertyballoon.com

Animal Adventure

Varysburg, NY

How about spending the day in an animal kingdom? You won't have to go to central Florida to find this Getaway. I found another hidden gem in our state...Hidden Valley Animal Adventure in Varysburg, Wyoming County.

This family-friendly destination brings you up close to an amazing array of exotic animals! After you jump aboard the Safari Trolley, you approach the tall, steel gates that slowly open for you to enter the 60-acre compound. It's like a scene from *Jurassic Park!* Hold on for an exciting guided ride through the countryside.

With admission, you get a cup of oats to feed the animals, and they know you've got food...they come right up to the trolley! There are more than 300 animals, but these animals aren't what you'd expect to see roaming around this part of Western New York! Zebra, camel, elk, ostrich..and many more! That's what makes this Getaway so unique. Bring your camera!

Hidden Valley Animal Adventure also has two restaurants, fine dining and a more casual bar & grill!

Hidden Valley Animal Adventure

2887 Royce Rd.
Varysburg, NY 14167

Info:

(585) 535-4100
www.hiddenvalleyadventure.com
Open Year Round
Safari Trolley Tours: May-October
Adults $18, Children (3-10) $14, Ages 2 and under free

Scan for map.
Learn how on page 5.

Travel Tip:

Even in Winter, you and your family can enjoy Hidden Valley Animal Adventure with 'Sleigh Rides!' Call ahead to book one for the holidays!

Antique Boat Museum

Clayton, NY

Heading to The 1000 Islands this summer doesn't mean you have to battle big crowds. This Getaway takes you to the small and quaint Village of Clayton, where you'll find one of the best kept secrets on the southern banks of the St. Lawrence River! Get ready to view over 300 beautifully preserved antique boats at The Antique Boat Museum!

After the indoor galleries, head outside to experience the gracious river lifestyle with a 30-minute on board tour of the 106-foot houseboat, *La Duchesse*! Built in 1903, she was custom made for hotelier George Boldt, manager of New York City's famed Waldorf-Astoria Hotel. The tour is included with your museum admission. The riverboat is not wheelchair accessible. The 4.5-acre campus also comes alive with speed boat races and boat shows, including the annual summer Antique Boat Show & Auction.

One of my favorite things to do on this Getaway is to take the thrilling 45-minute speed boat run through the islands aboard the beautiful *Miss T.I.*, open every day, every hour, between 10am and 4pm. Call ahead to register. It is worth the extra $25!

Antique Boat Museum

750 Mary Street
Clayton, NY 13624

Scan for map.
Learn how on page 5.

Info:

(315) 686-4104
www.abm.org
Open daily May thru October 9am-5pm.
Museum: Adults $13, Seniors (65+) $12, Military Active/Retired Free
Youth (6-17) $7, Ages 5 and under free.
Family $33 (2 adults, 2 children under 17)
Miss TI Ride :$25 for adults, $15 for children under 14
(Minimum of 2 adult passengers, maximum of 6 people per ride)
Museum and grounds are wheelchair accessible, excluding La Duchesse

Travel Tip:

Row a St. Lawrence Skiff for free! For a more tranquil experience on the water,
you can take a quiet row in this traditional classic on the protected waters of
French Creek Bay. Another unique experience at the Antique Boat Museum!

Art Museum

Who needs to go to New York City to see the masters of art? Come to Utica, New York to find a Getaway that is a huge surprise to many! The Munson Williams Proctor Museum of Art holds a renowned collection of art in 20 galleries, from 19th Century American Art to Modern & Contemporary. Come face to face with the greats, like Picasso, Georgia O'Keefe, Jackson Pollock, Andy Warhol, Thomas Cole and many more. Getting a good dose of culture never hurts!

One of the interesting little side trips from the main gallery is the walk down the glass corridor, leading to the historic Fountain Elms, a superbly restored 1850 Italianate mansion. You could spend a good 2 to 3 hours on this Museum Getaway. In the summer, there's art outside too, with the annual Sidewalk Art Show!

This Getaway is also very affordable because Admission and Parking are both free!

Munson Williams Proctor Museum of Art

310 Genesee Street
Utica, NY 13502

**Scan for map.
Learn how on page 5.**

Info:

(315) 797-0000
www.mwpai.org
Hours: Tuesday-Saturday 10 am-5pm,
Sunday 1pm-5pm, Closed Monday

Travel Tip:

You won't have to leave for lunch! Scrumptious sandwiches and wraps are available in the museum's Terrace Cafe'!

Ausable Chasm

Ausable Chasm, NY

This Getaway is one of my favorites, because it is the oldest natural attraction in North America! In the Adirondack region east of Lake Placid, along Route 9 near Lake Champlain, you'll discover what more than ten million visitors have discovered since it opened to the public in 1870...the amazing Ausable Chasm! You'll experience 5 miles of self-guided trails along breathtaking gorges and cliffs, descending hundreds of feet along natural stone walkways! There are trails for everyone... from the easiest 'Rim Walk', to the most challenging 'Cave and Falls Hike.' Be sure to wear good shoes and bring water! Plan to spend at least two to three hours on this Getaway.

Attraction...

At the end of the trail, when the water is high enough, be sure to take the exciting and scenic Raft Ride along the rapids of the Ausable River (ages 2 and up). A free trolley/shuttle will take you back to the welcome center.

Ausable Chasm
2144 Route 9
Ausable Chasm, NY 12911

Scan for map.
Learn how on page 5.

Info:
(518) 834-7454
www.ausablechasm.com
Open year round
Summer 9am-5pm
Fall, Winter, Spring, 9am-4pm
$16.95 Adults, $9.95 ages 5-12, under 5 are free!
Raft Ride- $12 Adults, $10 ages 5-12, $5 under age 5.

Travel Tip:
No pets or strollers are allowed in the chasm.

Bully Hill Vineyards

The view from way up here on the hill is crazy beautiful! Bully Hill Vineyards has been overlooking the south end of Keuka Lake for a very long time. Just 2 miles outside the quaint village of Hammondsport, Bully Hill is very much a village unto itself, with gift shops, a very good restaurant, wine tours, wine tastings, a museum and an art gallery! You could almost spend the entire day here!

Wine Tours are free and fun! They begin at the Visitor's Center with a guided walking tour of the estate and the unique history of its founder, Walter S. Taylor. Afterwards, a wine tasting!

Some of the wild and colorful labels on bottles of Bully Hill Wines come from the brush of Walter S. Taylor himself. Quite the artist! The art gallery here is filled with more than 200 of his originals! Also in the same complex, The Cooper Shop highlighting the early days of New York State wine making.

The restaurant! This is one of the big reasons I head up the hill! Great food with a great view, as you dine inside or outside. Sunday Brunch too! I suggest the Buffalo Burger!

Bully Hill Vineyards

8843 Greyton H Taylor Memorial Dr.
Hammondsport, NY 14840

Scan for map.
Learn how on page 5.

Info:
(607) 868-3610
www.bullyhill.com
Admission: Wine Tours free
Wine Tasting $5 with souvenir wine glass.
Open: Wine Shop / Tastings Daily 10am-5pm
Restaurant 11:30am - 4pm
(Call for dinner hours /lunch hours Nov.-April)
Museum/Art Gallery open daily 11am-5pm May-October
Closed Nov.-April.

Travel Tip:
While you're in the area, there is more to discover, like the Glenn Curtiss Aviation Museum and Keuka Lake boat tours on the beautiful Esperanza Rose in Branchport.

Caboose Motel

Avoca, NY

H ow about spending the night in an old caboose? You can, if you travel to Avoca, New York. A lot of people do! In fact, people from as far away as Australia have spent the night at the Caboose Motel, Route 415 in Steuben County.

On my travels, I've passed by this motel time after time and just had to stop! Five bright red cabooses from 1916 all lined up and furnished with bathroom and beds to accommodate 4 to 5 people each. And I've been told new mattresses are on the way! There's even an adjustable speaker in each caboose delivering the soothing sounds of a train headin' down the tracks as you drift off to sleep!

Just added...a new vending machine and laundry room for guests. Adding to that family feel, an outdoor wood campfire and play area, plus outside grills for guests! This is one of my favorite out-in-the-country Getaways because it is truly one-of-a-kind!

"A great getaway for the kids!"

Caboose Motel

60483 State Route 415
Avoca, NY 14809

Scan for map.
Learn how on page 5.

Info:

(607) 566-2216
www.caboosemotel.net
Open April-October
$80 plus tax / double occupancy, plus $7 per extra person

Travel Tip:

You'll be sleeping on the original bunks! These are not the most luxurious accommodations, but it's a fun time, especially for the kids!

Carrousel Museum

North Tonawanda, NY

Take a ride 15 minutes north of Buffalo to a forgotten street in North Tonawanda, to ride a classic carousel! Back in 1915, Thompson Street was home to The Herschell Carrousel Factory. It's still here! Today, the factory is a museum hosting about 15,000 visitors a year.

The star of the show? The actual 1916 Allan Herschell Carrousel in the original roadhouse! You get one ride with admission, and extra rides are only 50 cents each. Adding to the fun are exhibits of other amusement rides as well as self-guided and guided tours of the actual workshops where the original wooden carousel animals were carved and painted! The black and whites on the wall bring you *waaaay* back!

Another amazing thing they have here is the only remaining music roll production equipment from the Wurlitzer Company! Rolls and rolls of music! This is where that great carousel sound comes from!

To this day, many people, even some who live nearby, aren't even aware of this historical gem. It's an affordable family Getaway, where after an hour or two here, you'll understand the museum's motto: "Once Around is Never Enough!"

All photos courtesy of Herschell Carrousel Factory Museum

Herschell Carrousel Factory Museum

180 Thompson St.
North Tonawanda, NY 14120

Info:

(716) 693-1885

www.carrouselmuseum.org

Open April-December, daily in summer, closed Mondays and
Tuesdays in the spring and fall. Closed major holidays
$6 adults, $5 seniors, $3 children ages 2-16, under 2 are free.

Travel Tip:

Be sure to check out the children's gallery, where there is a small,
completely restored 1940s aluminum Kiddie Carousel! It was
created specifically for small children to ride, without the need
for adults to accompany them. The horses are child-size and
the machine moves more slowly than a full sized carousel.

**Scan for map.
Learn how on page 5.**

25

Catharine Cottages

Montour Falls, NY

If you're looking to get away from the rat race and yearn for peace and quiet, this Getaway in Montour Falls, Schuyler County, may be just what the doctor ordered... Spending a night or two in a cozy cottage!

I found Catharine Cottages along busy Route 14, just a few miles south of Watkins Glen. Set back from the road and noise, four clean, comfortable cottages provide a serene setting. The first thing you'll notice when you walk into your cottage is the smell of the wood that they were built from. They're pretty new! And just outside your front door, the soothing sounds of Catharine Creek!

I call this Getaway "camping without really camping!" After all, you do have a plush-top double bed, double futon couch, heat/AC, coffee maker, mini fridge, microwave and a shower! Throw into the mix your own fire pit, charcoal grill and a porch with chairs, and you've got rustic charm in the Finger Lakes! Bedding, linens and towels included. You even receive a Breakfast Basket of goodies when you arrive! Innkeeper Ilona will help you with everything!

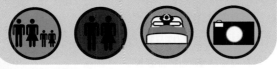

Catharine Cottages

2025 State Route 14
Montour Falls, NY 14865

Info:

(607) 535-0000
www.catharinecottages.com
$135 per night/double occupancy
Includes Breakfast Basket
Kids stay free!
4-person maximum per cabin. 2-night minimum on weekends.
No pets and no smoking in cottages
Open mid April - Mid November

Scan for map.
Learn how on page 5.

Travel Tip:

You're going to love how close you are to waterfalls!
Havana Glen Park nearby with a rugged trail and waterfalls,
Shequaga Falls right in Montour Falls. And the gem of the
Finger Lakes, Watkins Glen State Park! 19 spectacular waterfalls!

Classic Car Museum

How about more than 170 classic cars all in one place? That's exactly what you'll discover on this one-of-a-kind Getaway in Norwich, New York, Chenango County.

What I like most about this Getaway is walking in the unassuming building from the front, only to discover 5 huge, former factory buildings behind it, each filled with an incredible display of preserved and restored cars, one right after the other! This may be one of the best measures of American culture through automobile history in the Northeast. Another example of a hidden gem in our great state of New York!

The Northeast Classic Car Museum is family affordable and fully handicap accessible with scooters and wheelchairs available. Plan on spending about 2 hours there. Picture taking and video is permitted for non-commercial use only.

170 classic cars all in one place!

Northeast Classic
Car Museum
24 Rexford Street
State Route 23
Norwich, NY 13815

**Scan for map.
Learn how on page 5.**

Info:
(607) 334-2886

www.classiccarmuseum.org
Open 7 days a week from
9am-5pm - closed on major holidays
$9 Adults, $4 ages 6-18, under 6 Free

Travel Tip:
Keep an eye out for The Fabulous Franklins...a special
exhibit of cars manufactured in Syracuse from 1902 to 1934.

Crystal Lake Café

Interlaken, NY

What a story this Getaway has! A restaurant and a winery that both come from an unusual past. Americana Vineyards' tasting room is housed in a barn from the 1820's that originally came from 5 miles away! It was dismantled and rebuilt, found now on East Covert Road in Interlaken, off the Cayuga Wine Trail.

And right next to the barn, Crystal Lake Café. What began as a sandwich shop, has now become a full service restaurant with *from-scratch* food! The story goes...the place was only 'take-out', but people didn't want to leave! So now, you won't have to! Sit down and enjoy hand-packed burgers, house roasted turkey, homemade smoked sausages, BBQ pulled-pork and more! There's a reason the kitchen is as big as the vintage-furnished dining room: Chefs Jen and Lindsay require a lot of space to crank out some of the best food found in wine country! You know what they say...go where the locals go! And they all go here!

A great food find for wine trail enthusiasts, when you're hungry in the Finger Lakes.

Crystal Lake Café

4367 East Covert Road
Interlaken, NY 14847

Info:

(607) 387-6804
www.americanavineyards.com
Winery Hours: Mon. thru Sat. 10am-6pm Sun. 11am-6pm
Cafe Hours: Spring-Fall, open daily Mon-Wed. Noon-6pm,
Thurs. thru Sat. Noon-8pm., Sunday Brunch 11am-3pm
Dinner 4pm-8pm
Closed Mon.-Wed. starting November 1

**Scan for map.
Learn how on page 5.**

Travel Tip:

Sundays are awesome! Stop by the cafe for their famous Sunday
Brunch and Sunday Afternoon Concerts by local and traveling
musicians! A relaxing way to end your weekend!

Curtiss Museum

You can't miss this Getaway! Traveling down Route 54 in Hammondsport, the southern tip of Keuka Lake, look for the enormous 1949 C-46 Aircraft looming just outside of this gem in the Finger Lakes. This is the hometown of Glenn Curtiss, father of naval aviation! He is also known as the fastest man on earth! That's why you may see motorcycles when you first enter the museum. And there's so much more to see as you move through this giant house of history!

Glenn Curtiss Museum employees bubble-over with enthusiasm because of what they can share about this legendary hometown boy that did so much, more than 100 years ago. With this resumé, who could blame them!

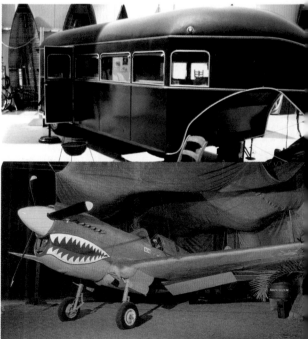

- He trained the first American female pilot, Rochestarian Blanche Stuart, in June, 1910.

- Curtiss flew the first pre-announced, officially observed flight in America with A.E.A. "June Bug", July 4, 1908.

- He invented the first flying boat! He used Keuka Lake as his runway!

All of his achievements are represented and proudly displayed in the Curtiss Museum! A great family Getaway!

Glenn Curtiss Museum

8419 State Route 54
Hammondsport, NY 14840

Scan for map.
Learn how on page 5.

Info:

(607) 569-2160
www.glennhcurtissmuseum.org
Adults $8.50, Seniors (65+) $7
Students (7-18) $5.50, ages 6 and under free.
Family Rate $25. Free Parking!
Wheelchair accessible. Open Year Round
May-Oct: Mon.-Sat. 9am-5pm, Sun. 10am-5pm
Nov-April: Mon.-Sun. 10am-4pm

Travel Tip:

While in Hammondsport, grab lunch! There are a variety of restaurants in the village and good food up the hill at Bully Hill Vineyards. The best view of Keuka Lake! Even a good Mexican restaurant, San Carlos, just a few miles south on Route 54 in Bath!

Elderberry Pond

Auburn, NY

A ride out into the countryside can sometimes lead to unique discoveries. And that's exactly what I found on a country road just east of Auburn, NY. The Restaurant at Elderberry Pond!

It all begins on a certified organic farm in the Finger Lakes region that produces fruits, vegetables, herbs, heritage pigs and chickens! Now, bring the creative expertise of professional chefs into a rustic, yet elegant setting with a dining room and outdoor patio overlooking the orchards, and you've got a fine dining experience! The menu features fresh produce, picked daily, and pasture-raised meats. People always talk about the potatoes! No wonder! They're freshly dug organic potatoes and you can really taste the difference!

If you're traveling through the Finger Lakes near Auburn and you've got an appetite for something special, pull over and make a call! Reservations are a must!

The Restaurant at Elderberry Pond

3712 Center Street Road
Auburn, NY 13021

Info:
(315) 252-6025
www.elderberrypond.com
Menu: Lunch Entrees $12-$13, Dinner Entrees $24-$32
Hours: Open Mid-March - December, Wednesday-Sunday
Lunch from 11:30am, Dinner from 5pm

Scan for map.
Learn how on page 5.

Travel Tip:
Don't miss the Country Food Store! Right next door to the restaurant is an old stone building once used back in the mid-1800's as a community pork rendering and smoke house. Today, farm produce and meats along with jams and jellies are for sale! It's even more festive in the Fall!

Elmira's Painted Lady

When in the the town where Huck Finn was born, do it up right and spend the night at Elmira's Painted Lady! Mark Twain spent 22 summers in Elmira. Some say he may have even visited this B&B Getaway! Situated in the Finger Lakes region, the rose-colored Victorian mansion on West Water Street has Twain-themed rooms, including a Mark Twain Suite. There's even a billiard room! A delicious 3-course gourmet breakfast is part of your overnight stay.

Owners Butch and Marilyn Monroe provide guests with brochures and maps of local attractions like Watkins Glen, the Corning Museum of Glass and many Finger Lakes wineries! Also, new at the inn....hot air balloon rides!

Serenity, surrounded by fun things to do!

Elmira's Painted Lady B&B

520 W. Water Street
Elmira, NY 14905

Scan for map.
Learn how on page 5.

Info:
(607) 846-3500
www.elmiraspaintedlady.com
Open year round
From $130/night based on double occupancy

Travel Tip:
You can walk to Mark Twain's study nearby on the Elmira College Campus! Grab a Mark Twain map there to find all things Mark Twain in Elmira, including his final resting place in Woodlawn Cemetery.

Erie Canal Village

Rome, NY

This outdoor Getaway is a living museum that has New York State written all over it!

Erie Canal Village in Rome, N.Y. is a reconstructed 19th century settlement, and it's where the first shovelful of earth was turned in 1817 for the construction of the original Erie Canal.

The village is home to three important museums that will help take you back in time. The Harden Museum houses fantastic horse-drawn vehicles. The Erie Canal Museum tells the story of the Erie Canal's beginning. And the New York State Museum of Cheese, the former Merry and Weeks Cheese Factory, was brought here from nearby Verona, N.Y.

You'll wander the grounds passing people in period clothing on their way to many 19th century structures like Bennett's Tavern, a Blacksmith Shop with demonstrations, The Ice House, Wood Creek School and beautiful Victorian homes. You can even take a train ride alongside the Erie Canal in the 12-ton, 1956 Plymouth DDT Diesel!

Affordable and fun! Erie Canal Village, a good Central New York summertime, family Getaway. Hey! A little history never hurt!

Erie Canal Village

Scan for map.
Learn how on page 5.

5789 Rome New London Road
(Routes 46 & 49)
Rome, NY 13440

Info:
(315) 337-3999
www.eriecanalvillage.net
Adults $6.50, Seniors (55+) $5, Children (6-17) $4
Ages 5 and under are free.
Train Rides - Adults $5, Seniors $4, Children $3
5 and under free.
Open from last week of May through end of August
Wed-Sat 10am to 5pm, Closed Sunday, Monday and Tuesday

Travel Tip:
Be sure to pack a lunch! There's an open air picnic area
and covered pavillion.

Fort Rickey

Rome, NY

This family Getaway is more than a zoo! Fort Rickey Children's Discovery Zoo in Rome, New York is one of our state's hidden gems, designed to give kids a closer experience with animals! In fact, their mission statement is all about gentle interaction with wild animals...to become people who care about protecting wildlife.

And you'll know there's wildlife on this getaway when you hear the howling of wolves! The Wolves Exhibit may be the most popular part of this Getaway where owner, Len Cross, actually gets inside the enclosed area with 2 wolves and conducts a presentation explaining why it is safe for him to do this! It's a huge crowd pleaser!

The Maternity Ward is also a special area that gives children a chance to hold baby animals. Kids can also feed many of the animals at the Discovery Zoo. It's encouraged!

If you want a family experience in a beautiful, open field minus all the cages, this Getaway is perfect!

Fort Rickey Children's Discovery Zoo

5135 Rome-London Road
Rome, NY 13440

Info:

(315) 336-1930
www.fortrickey.com
Adults $9.95, Children $6.95
Seniors $8.50
Under 2 are free
Open mid May through End of October
Spring-daily 10am-4pm, Summer-daily 10am-5pm.

Scan for map.
Learn how on page 5.

Travel Tip:

Save some money by going to their web site for
your Free Child Pass!

Goat Island

Niagara Falls, NY

If I want to see Niagara Falls up close, I go to Goat Island, Niagara Falls USA! In fact, this may be the best place to see the falls! Many gather out on Terrapin Point for the best view. You are so close to the falls, it's startling! The island is literally surrounded by the American's side Bridal Veil Falls and the Canadian's side Horseshoe Falls.

Goat Island is pretty big, so to save you some time, you can jump on board the Niagara Scenic Trolley! For just a couple of bucks, the ride will take you out to Three Sisters Islands, putting you very close to the rapids just above the Horseshoe Falls. It's beautiful out there! Caution! It may be tempting to wade in the waters, but it's not a good idea to take the chance!

So, if you're bringing your friends to see Niagara Falls for the first time, Goat Island is an excellent way to do it! *Falls Fact...Goat Island is the oldest State Park in the USA!*

Goat Island
Niagara Falls, NY

Info:
(716) 278-1796
www.niagarafallsstatepark.com
Goat Island Parking, Lot # 2- $10 per car.
Open Year Round
Cave of the Winds- Adults $11, Children (6-12) $8, 42" tall requirement.
Maid of the Mist - Adults $15.50, Children (6-12) $9
ages 5 and under free

Scan for map.
Learn how on page 5.

Travel Tip:
Goat Island has 2 intense Niagara Falls experiences! Cave of the Winds takes you down below to the base of the Bridal Veil Falls! Nowhere else on Earth gets you closer to the falls! Maid of the Mist is an amazing boat excursion on the mighty Niagara up close to the Horseshoe Falls! Even with your souvenir rain poncho...you'll still get wet!

43

Green Lakes

Green Lakes State Park, just east of Syracuse in Fayetteville, NY, is one of those places a lot of people have yet to visit. But once you do, you're hooked! Especially if you like green and blue!

The 2 glacial lakes in the park, described as meromictic lakes, make this Getaway very unique. Here's the deal...there is no fall and spring mixing of surface and bottom waters, which gives the lakes a high potential for evidence of ancient plant and animal life. This also gives the lakes their special color of green and blue. You've never seen anything like it!

There is a pretty nice beach on Green Lake with access to fishing, hiking, swimming, a playground and a snack bar. Nearby Round Lake is a Natural National Landmark. There's no swimming allowed, however, the running and walking trail around the entire lake is a perfect alternative!

In addition to the lakes, there is the 18-hole Robert Trent Jones golf course complete with restaurant in the clubhouse. There are also camping and cabin sites.

credit: NYS OPRHP

credit: NYS OPRHP

Green Lakes State Park

7900 Green Lakes Road
Fayetteville, NY 13066

Scan for map.
Learn how on page 5.

Info:
(315) 637-6111
www.nysparks.com/parks/172
Park Fee: $8 per car.
Swimming included in entrance fee
Row Boat Rental $5 per hour
Open Year Round
Beach Swimming Late May-August. Fishing only on Green Lake.
Household pets are not allowed in the bathing areas, but can
be brought into the park while kept on a leash.

Travel Tip:
Seniors...NYS residents 62 or older get FREE weekday
access to state parks, with valid NYS drivers license.

Harriet Tubman Home

Auburn, NY

This Getaway is all about one very courageous woman, Harriet Tubman. After the Civil War, she settled in Auburn on South Street, thanks to the encouragement of her friend, William Seward. The home she built for aged African Americans, is today, a remarkable place to visit!

The home preserves the legacy of "The Moses of Her People" in the place where she lived and died, a free woman. The site is located on 26 acres of land, just south of town. The Harriet Tubman Home was almost demolished in 1944, but a fund drive raised enough money for restoration and on April 13, 1953, the home was dedicated as a memorial to Tubman's life and work. Some articles of furniture and a portrait that belonged to Tubman are now on display in the home.

Harriet Tubman's life of leading dozens of slaves to freedom, now leads visitors from all around to this historically important Getaway. Not to be missed on your day trip to Auburn!

credit: Kristian Reynolds

Harriet Tubman Home
180 South Street
Auburn, NY 13021

Info:
(315) 252-2081
www.historyshometown.com
www.tourcayuga.com
Adults $4.50, Seniors & College Students $3, Youth 5-17 $2.50
Open February 1-October 31, Tues-Fri 10am-4pm, Sat 10am-3pm
Last tour begins 1 hour before close
November 1-January 31 By appointment only
Visitor's Center is handicapped accessible
The 'Home' requires assistance with 2 steps

Scan for map.
Learn how on page 5.

Travel Tip:
Fort Hill Cemetery is a beautiful place to visit. Set on a hill overlooking Auburn, it is Harriet Tubman's final resting place. Set among majestic trees, this historical site is a peaceful place to come when in Auburn. William H. Seward is buried here, too!

Herkimer Diamond Mines

Herkimer, NY

On this Getaway, you're going to have to wear goggles and carry a crack hammer! You are about to be a prospector for the day at Herkimer Diamond Mines! You won't actually be finding diamonds but, if you're lucky, beautiful double-terminated quartz crystals that look and shine like diamonds. They say these geometrically shaped stones are close to 5-hundred million years old! The thrill comes when you crack open a rock and there it is! Keep all that you find!

After a hard day at the mines, you may want to browse the gift shop with 5000 square feet of jewelry, gems and rocks & minerals from every continent! Don't forget the museum upstairs! Right across the street from the mines, there's a KOA Kampground for tents, trailers and RV hookups. Comfy cabins are available with a playground and swimming pool!

Fascinating Fact...a Herkimer Diamond cluster in the formation of a cross was found the morning of September 11, 2001, at The Herkimer Diamond Mines! The most beautiful discovery here ever!

Herkimer Diamond Mines

4601 State Route 28
Herkimer, NY 13350

Scan for map.
Learn how on page 5.

Info:

(315) 717-0175
(315) 891-7355 (weekends/evenings)
KOA Kampground Reservations
(315) 891-7355 or (800) 562-0897
www.herkimerdiamond.com
Ages 13 and up $11, Children (5-12) $9, ages 4 and under free
Admission includes all day prospecting and the use of a rock hammer.
Diamond Mines & KOA Kampgrounds:
Open daily mid April–October, 9am-5pm

Travel Tip:

If you're mining, be sure to wear boots and use sun screen!
Also, take a bottle or two of water! It can get hot out there!

Hermann J. Wiemer Vineyard

Dundee, NY

On a crisp fall afternoon, I found myself holding on tightly as I was taken on a bumpy motorized-cart ride up into the original vineyards at Hermann J. Wiemer Vineyards, in the Finger Lakes. A pretty amazing sight up there, overlooking the western shores of Seneca Lake!

On this Getaway, you won't necessarily be up among the vines and grapes, however, you'll be down below, inside a renovated 90-year old barn. Thanks to an award-winning team of Cornell architects, the barn has been transformed into a wonderful mix of bare wooden walls, cathedral-like ceilings with white chandeliers and Italian stainless steel tanks. The surroundings are as tastefully done as the wine itself! This is the wine production area, tasting facility and retail wine shop.

Chardonnays, Reds, Sparkling Wines...but it's the Rieslings! Harvesting grapes by hand, the old-fashioned way, is what makes this Getaway so special. Many wine experts consider this winery's Rieslings some of the best in the United States!

Hermann J. Wiemer Vineyard

3962 Route 14
Dundee, NY 14837

**Scan for map.
Learn how on page 5.**

Info:

(607) 243-7971
www.wiemer.com
Admission: Wine Tastings $3
Open: Retail Shop / Tasting Room
Monday-Saturday 10am-5pm, Sunday 11am-5pm
Subject to change January-March. Call ahead.

Travel Tip:

Be sure to check the events page on the Wiemer website!
You may want to plan around these exciting tastings and
concerts.

Home of FDR

This Getaway takes you 70 miles south of Albany to Hyde Park, New York to discover a home along the Hudson River that is one of our state's most popular historical landmarks. Springwood, the Home of Franklin D. Roosevelt! You begin the Getaway at the Visitor Center, where you can take in a brief film that helps you get acquainted. This is where you'll organize your ranger-led guided tour. Then, it's off to FDR's lifelong home! You can almost feel the presidential gravity as you approach. Once inside the home, you'll be amazed at the history! Ask questions, your guide has so much to share!

Your tour also includes the very first Presidential Library, which opened to the public in 1941. Franklin Roosevelt was a great collector! The library holds more than 34,000 items! Self-guided tours here also include the Museum, which is a must see!

Note: The first floor of the FDR Home is handicap accessible. Check website for lift availability to 2nd floor.

"All that is within me cries out to go back to my home on the Hudson River"

- FDR

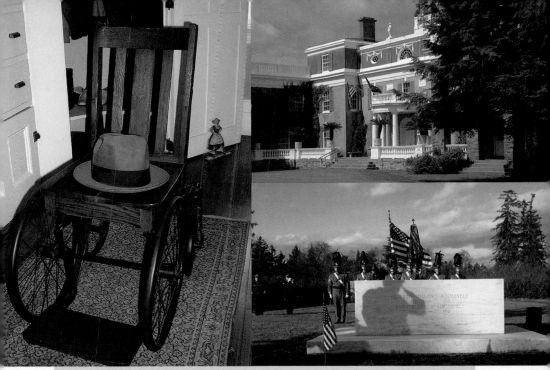

FDR Home
4097 Albany Post Road
Hyde Park, NY 12538

**Scan for map.
Learn how on page 5.**

Info:
(845) 229-5320
www.nps.gov/hofr
Open year round
7 days a week - 9am-5pm
Closed major holidays
$14 per person, Ages 15 and under are free!

Travel Tip:
While you're on the beautiful 300-acre grounds, make a point to walk over to the resting place of our only 4-term president and his wife, Eleanor.

Hot Air Balloon

We all love that Sunday afternoon road-trip in October to take in the colors of Fall. This Getaway goes one better by seeing Mother Nature's best from high above in a hot air balloon! Spring, summer or fall, Balloons Over Letchworth makes this one of my favorite getaways in New York State!

As the balloon fills and rises, it begins to lift you higher and higher, eventually to 500 feet off the ground. You'll quickly realize this is like no other experience! You'll be amazed at how peaceful, quiet and calm it is way up there. What makes this particular hot air balloon ride most unique, and even more intense, is the flight literally OVER Letchworth State Park! Incredibly breathtaking!

Never fear...friend and trusty pilot Sean Quigley, with more than 25 years of experience and expertise, makes your ride very comfortable. Sean's skill taking the balloon down into the gorge and back out again makes this Getaway even more spectacular!

The landing? Just as exciting as take off! And half the fun is pitching in to help load the balloon back into the truck. All in all, this hot air balloon ride is a Getaway you won't forget!

Balloons Over Letchworth

Letchworth State Park

Scan for map.
Learn how on page 5.

Info:
(585) 493-3340

www.balloonsoverletchworth.com

$245 Per Person

Balloon Flights are at sunrise and sunset, 7 days a week, weather permitting. Launch site between middle and upper falls area near Glen Iris Inn. Park entrance fee.

Open May-October

Travel Tip:
Escape the $8 State Park entry fee when you arrive before 9am or after 5pm! And...The Glen Iris Inn will pay your entrance fee when you dine or stay overnight at the inn!

Inn at Gothic Eves

If you're looking for a warm and cozy place to spend a night or two, consider my B&B pick in the Village of Trumansburg, N.Y...The Inn at Gothic Eves!

As you travel down East Main Street nearing #112, the first thing you'll notice is the wonderful architecture of this historic 1855 inn. And inside the inn, it's just as beautiful! Perfect for an overnight stay any time of year, but in the winter months, there's special charm if you score a room with a fireplace! Eight beautifully decorated guest rooms with period furnishings, fine linens and access to an enormous outdoor hot tub! Spa services are available too! The inn's Finger Lakes location is also perfect, on the Cayuga Wine Trail and very close to Taughannock Falls State Park. Ithaca is only 10 minutes away!

Breakfast? This may be the most memorable part of your stay! Local, organic, fresh and delicious! All included in your room rate!

If you're looking for a quiet getaway for just the 2 of you, this is it! Innkeeper Rose will take very good care of you!

Inn at Gothic Eves photo credits: Elizabeth Campbell/Jumping Rocks Photography

The Inn at Gothic Eves
112 East Main Street
Trumansburg, NY 14886

Info:
(607) 387-6033
www.gothiceves.com
B&B Starting Rates: $189-$269
Open Year Round

Scan for map.
Learn how on page 5.

Travel Tip:
If you're hankering for pizza...you are in luck! People come from far away to New York Pizzeria in T-Burg. Fabrizio hand-tosses the dough the old-fashioned way to make his authentic, thin crust pizza! Hours can vary and are sometimes unpredictable but if they're open...go in and grab a slice...or 2!
2 W. Main Street
(607) 387-3700

Jellystone Park

North Java, NY

Yogi Bear is alive and well! So is Boo Boo! You'll find them in North Java, Western New York, at one of my very favorite family campgrounds, Jellystone Park! This Getaway is 100 acres of peaceful pines in a friendly atmosphere of families getting away for the weekend, or on vacation.

Pretty much any way you want to go camping, Yogi and the gang have you covered! Bring your tents or hookup your camper trailer or RV. They even have lake cabins, deluxe cabins and chalet accommodations, all to rent. My choice? The Lake Cabins! I love the view, the charcoal BBQ grill and fire ring for s'mores at night! You can even rent a golf cart to get around!

Here's what else makes this a perfect family Getaway: unlimited use of Yogi Bear's Water Zone! A 16,000 square foot, multi-level, interactive water playground with waterslides, a fort, water cannon and more! Other fun includes kayaks, canoes, mini-golf, laser tag and pedal karts. And all of this is included in your rate!

With street names like Pic-A-Nic Walkway and Ranger Smith Lane, you just know this is going to be fun! As they say here..."*Where You Camp With Friends!*"

Jellystone Park of WNY

5204 Youngers Road
North Java, NY 14113

Info:
(585) 457-9644
www.wnyjellystone.com
Campsite and rental units vary in
price depending on number of days
and time of year
Open Spring, Summer and Fall

Scan for map.
Learn how on page 5.

Travel Tip:
Be sure to check the events page on the Jellystone website!
Every week there's something new and exciting going
on, so you may want to plan your stay around the fun
themes they have.

Journey Behind the Falls

Niagara Falls, ON, Canada

credit: Niagara Parks Commission

Head to the Canadian side of Niagara Falls for this wet and wild Getaway! Journey Behind the Falls gives you a view of this natural wonder of the world like no other!

Once you cross the Rainbow Bridge to Canada, head south on the Niagara Parkway and look for the Table Rock Welcome Centre. It is in this complex that you'll find the elevator that'll take you down 150 feet through bedrock, eventually to underground tunnels. You'll need your souvenir, biodegradable poncho for this one! You are literally at the foot of the Horseshoe Falls with wind and water against your body from the falls thundering down, 13 stories above! And if that isn't enough....follow the tunnels to 2 portals, openings behind the falls! What a view!

This Getaway is wheelchair accessible except for the lower observation deck. Remember! When traveling into Canada, you must have a current passport or enhanced driver's license. Children 15 and under should have an original birth certificate.

credit: Niagara Parks Commission

Journey Behind the Falls

6650 Niagara Parkway
Niagara Falls, ON, Canada

**Scan for map.
Learn how on page 5.**

Info:

(905) 354-1551
www.niagaraparks.com
Open year round
Hours differ, see website
Adults $15.95
Children $10.95 (6-12)
5 and under free! (Canadian Dollars, plus tax)

Travel Tip:

Summer is a very busy time at the Falls, so plan to be here early in
the day. Unless you like long lines, avoid Labor Day Weekend!

Judge Ben Wiles

Skaneateles, NY

All aboard the *Judge Ben Wiles*! This is a classic wood-trimmed steel boat, named after a Syracuse bankruptcy judge from long ago, now cruising Skaneateles Lake. I still consider this lake as one of the most beautiful in the Finger Lakes! Easy to get to on Route 20, just east of Auburn, N.Y.

On a day trip to this bustling village, the 50-minute sightseeing cruise on the *Judge Ben Wiles* is a perfect middle-of-the-day idea. My favorite part of this boating adventure is the outstanding view of the homes, mansions and history of the area. You wouldn't normally get to see any of this from land!

Tickets for the sightseeing cruise can be obtained at the office, a block from the dock in Skaneateles. Add a little romance to your day with one of their Dinner Cruises! This Getaway also has special events like Pirate Day in August and a Full Moon Cruise each month. All cruises are weather permitting.

The Barbara S. Wiles

Judge Ben Wiles

Judge Ben Wiles

11 Jordan St., PO Box 61
Skaneateles, NY 13152

Info:

(315) 685-8500
www.midlakesnav.com
Sightseeing Cruise $12/person
Dinner Cruise $50 per person
Season runs Mid-May through
End of September
Cruises are daily and times vary

Scan for map.
Learn how on page 5.

Travel Tip:

Be adventurous and navigate your own Lockmaster along the Erie Canal! Your boat comes complete with beds, a kitchen and bikes! An amazing way to explore towns and trails on this wonderful New York State waterway! Check it out on the Mid-Lakes Navigation website!

Martin's Fantasy Island

Grand Island, NY

Where else are you going to find an old-fashioned Western Shoot Out?! That's just one of the things that puts this Getaway in the *classic amusement park* category! A cleverly choreographed Wild West drama in Westerntown is a rare sight you won't likely find anywhere else. It happens 4 times a day at Martin's Fantasy Island, on Grand Island, just north of Buffalo. This has been a summertime family Getaway since 1961!

If you're a parent who likes to see your kids grow up the way you did, this should do it! Fantasy Island has held onto the classic rides you don't see at a lot of the newer parks. Who doesn't love a classic wooden coaster? The Silver Comet still delivers! And hold on, this one moves! To cover all ages, Martin's Fantasy Island also offers a variety of kids rides in Kiddie Land, a lake for canoeing and a pretty big Water Park with slides, wave pool and lazy river.

The months of May and September bring off-season pricing and free parking, making it a very affordable Amusement Park Getaway for the family!

Martin's Fantasy Island

2400 Grand Island Blvd.
Grand Island, NY 14072

Scan for map.
Learn how on page 5.

Info:

(716) 773-7591
www.martinsfantasyisland.com
Open May-September with varying hours
Closed Mondays except Memorial Day and Labor Day
Waterpark opens in June
48"and over $25.95, Under 48" $20.95, After 5pm and Off
Season $14.95. Seniors $17.95, After 5pm and Off Season $14.95
Children 2 and under free. Admission includes unlimited use of
rides, shows and canoes.

Travel Tip:

Be sure to check the "Special Offers" page on their website for
discounts and events!

Mountain Horse Farm
B&B and Spa
Naples, NY

There are a lot of Bed and Breakfasts out there but the one I found, secluded in the Bristol hills near Naples, New York, is just my style. Mountain Horse Farm B&B and Spa is contemporary and luxurious, yet a bit rustic, fitting in perfectly in the heart of the Finger Lakes.

Over 30 acres of peace and quiet! There are 2 guest rooms in the Lodge that have a wrap-around porch, for great viewing of the horses. The 4 guest rooms in the new Carriage House and Spa facility are a bit larger, with fireplaces! Rooms are decorated in warm colors and furnished with quality bedding and locally handcrafted wooden furniture! And to pamper yourself, 2 deluxe side-by-side massage tables, perfect for couples! They also offer an infrared sauna, aroma therapy and yoga.

Innkeeper Suzanne Vullers creates an absolutely delicious breakfast, included with your room rate. Recommendations are offered for dinner in the village of Naples nearby. Guests are also close to Bristol Mountain Ski Resort and Finger Lakes wine trails.

If you're looking for a great couples Getaway where you can really get away from it all, this may be it! Also, think 'girlfriends weekend!'

Mountain Horse Farm B&B and Spa

7520 West Hollow Rd.
Naples, NY 14512

Info:

(585) 374-5056
www.mountainhorsefarm.com
Open year round
Call or book online
Room rates from $135 to $220
per night / double occupancy
Breakfast included
Many theme packages, including spa packages, are offered!

Scan for map.
Learn how on page 5.

Travel Tip:

Bring your adventure hat! Mountain Horse Farm has three miles of groomed trails that guests can use for hiking, snowshoeing and cross-country skiing!

Mountain Coaster

Imagine a Getaway on an outdoor coaster...in the middle of winter! I found a great one at The Adventure Center at Greek Peak Mountain Resort in Cortland, NY. Bringing on more attractions at ski resorts in the non-skiing months seems to be the new trend, but this coaster Getaway is great all year long!

You'll experience 4,300 feet of pure excitement on a two-person car, independently controlled by you! Take it slow and steady as you soak in the scenery, or make an exhilarating descent through the forest at speeds up to 28 miles per hour! Use your hand brakes lightly when you need to, or let it out completely and get the full downhill thrill! My advice in the winter is to use a scarf to cover your face; it can be a very brisk ride!

Nor'easter Mountain Coaster at Greek Peak

2000 New York 392
Cortland, NY 13045

Scan for map.
Learn how on page 5.

Info:
(800) 955-2754
www.greekpeakmtnresort.com
www.cascadesindoorwaterpark.com
Open all year, Tuesday, Thursday,
Friday 12pm-7pm. Saturday,
Sunday 10am-7pm. Closed Mondays and Wednesdays
Coaster is $10 per ride / $49 Unlimited.
Rider must be 54" tall to ride alone, at least 3 years old 38" tall
to ride with companion 16 years or older.
To ride double, one rider must be 54" and 16 years old.
Maximum combined weight of 350 pounds per car.

Travel Tip:
After a day of winter fun outdoors, take in more than 500 feet of water slides
indoors! The resort also has Cascades Indoor Water Park, where it's always
84 degrees! Check their website for combo specials!

Olcott Beach Carousel Park

One of my favorite rides is along the Lake Ontario State Parkway: the Seaway Trail, out of Rochester, continuing west on Route 18 into Niagara County. Scenic and beautiful with orchards and fruit stands along the way. And, other than an occasional hay wagon, not a lot of traffic! When you reach the Hamlet of Olcott Beach, be ready to go back in time just like generations of people before you. The old amusement park may be gone, but a new park has appeared. This is where you'll find Olcott Beach Carousel Park. Perfect for families!

The kids will want to ride all 5 vintage, fully restored classics, including the 1928 style Herschell-Spillman 2-row Carousel! The 1931 Wurlitzer band organ completes the experience! This is a nice, small park, all run by friendly community volunteers. The cost is also reminiscent of the 40's and 50's! All rides...only 25 cents! And you still buy your tickets from the lady in the ticket booth! Add free park admission and free parking and you've got a very affordable family Getaway!

As they say here at Olcott Beach Carousel Park, *Building Memories for a New Generation!*

credit:
Wayne Peters

Olcott Beach Carousel Park

5979 Main Street
Olcott, NY 14126

Info:

(716) 778-7066
www.olcottbeachcarouselpark.org
Free Admission and free parking
Rides 25 cents each
Kiddy ride height requirement 52 inches tall or less!
Open Memorial Weekend (Sat., Sun., Mon. 12pm-6pm)
Weekends in June (Sat. 12pm-8pm, Sun. 12pm-6pm)
July - Labor Day (Wed-Sunday 12pm-6pm, until 8pm on Saturdays)

Scan for map.
Learn how on page 5.

Travel Tip:

Not far from the park on Route 18, look for Thirty Mile Point
Lighthouse in Golden Hill State Park, in Barker, N.Y. Take the 70-
foot spiral staircase to the top for an outstanding view!

Pollywogg Holler

Belmont, NY

It takes a bit of doing to find Pollywogg Holler! It's supposed to! Hidden out in the foothills of the Allegheny Mountains, what began as a one-cabin creation is now an entire multi-cabin eco-resort in Belmont, N.Y. This is a very rustic Getaway in a setting of wooded, natural beauty, Adirondack-style craftsmanship, solar electricity, organic gardening and gravity fed spring water! Talk about going green!

A winding trail through the woods, past sculptures and a geodesic dome takes adventurous guests to the Main Lodge. This is where you leave your hectic life behind! Spending the night includes dinner and breakfast! From the Sauna Loft to the Sugar Shack, to the hobbit-like twisting staircase up to the Wood Loft, the accommodations are each a bit different. This is not luxurious 5-star lodging, and not for everyone! But, if you're looking for a unique experience in the woods, this Getaway may be for you!

Pollywogg Holler

6240 South Road
Belmont, NY 14813

Info:

(585) 268-5292
www.pollywoggholler.com
Beginning at $115 per person / per night
Rate includes breakfast and dinner
Open Year Round by reservation
No pets

**Scan for map.
Learn how on page 5.**

Travel Tip:

Can't spend the night? Come by for just a visit, Wednesdays
5pm-9pm and Sundays 1pm-6pm. Barb & Bill Castle and
family would love to show you around their hidden creation!
Bring a flashlight!

Renaissance Festival

Sterling. NY

Getting to this Getaway takes some doing. If it seems as if you are driving out in the middle of nowhere, beyond modern civilization...you are! Heck, this Getaway takes you back to the year 1585! But, oh what fun! You've made it to The Renaissance Festival weekend summer celebration in Sterling, New York!

Every summer, for just a handful of weekends, you get to enjoy more than 100 stage and street performers recreating an authentic English Renaissance Village. From Pirate Invasion to Highland Fling, each summer weekend has a special theme. Many visitors who come to roam the cool, wooded landscape also dress up Renaissance-style, so it's hard to tell the performers from the guests! My favorite attraction is Tomato Justice, where guests hurl tomatoes at a restrained rogue! Hilarious! This day-long experience is very realistic, so bring the kids. They'll be learning something and won't even know it!

Ranked #3 out of more than 300 festivals in North America in 2011, The Sterling Renaissance Festival experience is worth the one-hour drive east out of Rochester. A good time for all!

Sterling Renaissance Festival

15385 Farden Rd.
Sterling, NY 13156

Info:

(315) 947-5782
www.sterlingfestival.com
Open Weekends
July - Mid August
10am-7pm
Adults $25.95, Children (6-12) $15.95
Free parking.

Scan for map.
Learn how on page 5.

Travel Tip:

Come hungry...extreme Renaissance food awaits! Steak on a Spear, Mile High Chocolate Cake and the famous Giant Turkey Legs! Fine Feasting for all!

Rock City Park

Olean, NY

You won't believe what I found in the Enchanted Mountains of Cattaraugus County! Rocks...big rocks! Rock City Park is an amazing outdoor getaway, just south of Olean, New York. This fascinating natural wonder will take you back in time millions of years! After descending a mysterious metal staircase, you enter another world of unusual rock formations along easy trails that take you in between, around and underneath giant boulders! My favorite? Balancing Rock! A 1000-ton boulder that seems to defy gravity! Bring along a camera, a bottle of water and good walking or hiking shoes!

There is a big souvenir gift shop including many types of gems, minerals and rocks from all over the world. Rest rooms are available.

If you're looking for a good family adventure, Rock City Park is it!

Attraction...
Talk about going back in time!
Be sure to see the Museum!

Rock City Park has been open to visitors since 1890!

Rock City Park

505 Route 16 South
Olean, NY 14760

Info:

(716) 372-7790
(866) 404-ROCK (7625)
www.rockcitypark.com
Open May 1-October 31
9am-6pm Daily
$4.50 Adults, $2.75 (Ages 6-12), Seniors $3.75 (62+)
Ages 5 and under free!
Group discounts

Scan for map.
Learn how on page 5.

Travel Tip:

Bring lunch! There are picnic tables!

Sackets Harbor

Sackets Harbor, NY

credit: OPRHP-BHS – Rich Clauss

The words 'quaint' and 'peaceful' come to mind when you first turn the corner into the Village of Sackets Harbor. You'll see flowers in bloom and shaded sidewalks that lead all the way to the end of Main Street. The history of Sackets Harbor really gets good as you approach the battlefields. If you forgot your history lesson on the War of 1812 in school...this will be a nice refresher!

Sackets Harbor in Jefferson County, just west of Watertown, was founded in 1801 by Augustus Sackett. The US Navy built a major shipyard and headquarters here, while the Army constructed forts and barracks. Today, you'll get to tour the important battlefields on the shores of Lake Ontario. You'll also be able to take in the art galleries, good restaurants, antique shops and stores. For overnight, there's a decent selection of hotels and B&B's.

Don't be surprised by the occasional golf cart whizzing by! These are tours being conducted for those who enjoy a good dose of area history. Sackets Harbor makes for a great day-trip, or make a weekend of it on your way to the Thousand Islands! Take Exit # 42 off I-81 North!

creadit: OPRHP-SHBSHS

Sackets Harbor, NY

Scan for map.
Learn how on page 5.

Info:

(315) 646-2321
www.sacketsharborNY.com
Battlefields are open dawn to dusk
Year-round at no charge
Historic Site. Buildings open in May.
$3 General, $2 Seniors, $2 Military, $2 Students, 12 and under free.

Travel Tip:

Hungry? My favorite place to eat is at the Tin Pan Galley, 110 W.
Main. Great food, especially their big breakfasts! Ask to
sit outside in their Patio Garden. Seasonal, closed
Monday and Tuesday. Call ahead for lunch/dinner.
(315) 646-3812. Mmmm! Stuffed French Toast!

Seabreeze

Rochester, NY

We all love the big amusement parks, but it's the small classics that have the nostalgia. At Seabreeze Amusement Park, that includes a pretty intense original wooden coaster ride on the Jack Rabbit! It's especially wild at night!

Seabreeze Amusement Park on the shores of Lake Ontario, north of Rochester, has been here amusing summertime crowds since the 1800's! The Jack Rabbit isn't the only classic ride here. The Carousel! The Bumper Cars! The Flyers! I remember my Dad taking me on the Log Flume as a kid. This classic is still, to this day, creating screams and getting people wet on that final drop! Fast forward in time to today's way to get wet at their impressive Waterpark. Inner Tube Slides, High Speed Hydro Racer, Wave Pool, Lazy River and Kiddie Slides too. For the ultimate waterpark experience...try the Helix! Old and new combined for exciting summertime fun, now that's a family Getaway!

Seabreeze Amusement Park

4600 Culver Rd
Rochester, NY 14622

Scan for map.
Learn how on page 5.

Info:
(585) 323-1900
www.seabreeze.com
Free Parking
Ages 2 and under Free
Open Mid-May through Mid-September
Spring 11am-9pm various days, Summer 11am-10pm daily
Ride & Slide Pass $27.99, Under 48" Pass $22.99
Night Rider Pass (After 5pm) $19.99, Spectator Pass $11.99
Check on-line calender for daily schedules and closed days

Travel Tip:
Buy tickets online to save a few bucks and avoid those long
lines at the park entrance!

Seneca Park Zoo

Rochester, NY

I am all about family Getaways. And the Seneca Park Zoo in Rochester is definitely a family Getaway! Every single age group will find something to enjoy here! The grounds are easy to stroll at a slow, casual pace, and there are so many wonderful things to see along the way.

Photo credit: Matthew Burroughs

Photo credit: Debra Wallace

The zoo's state-of-the-art *Step Into Africa* exhibit is a huge hit! See the amazing elephants and beautiful lions! For nose-to-nose underwater viewing, head to the Rocky Coasts! Here, you'll see the black-footed penguins, seemingly playful polar bears and entertaining sea lions. There are hands-on exhibits for kids and a ton of educational events throughout the year, like Wonders of Water and Elephant Awareness Day. They've even thought of the 21 and over crowd with Zoo Brew and Party Madagascar!

It's hard to believe how much the Seneca Park Zoo has grown over the years. If you haven't visited in a while, you'll be pleasantly surprised. What a fun day trip!

Photo credit: Hugh Scolton

Seneca Park Zoo

2222 St. Paul Street
Rochester, NY 14621

**Scan for map.
Learn how on page 5.**

Info:

(585) 336-7200
www.senecaparkzoo.org
Open Year Round
Jan. 1-March 31/ Nov. 1- Dec. 31 (10am-3pm)
Adults $9, seniors $8, ages 3-11 $6
April 1 - Oct. 31 (10am-4pm)
Adults $11, seniors $10, ages 3-11 $8.
Ages 2 and under free
Open until 7pm on Tuesdays in summer

Travel Tip:

For working families who want to enjoy a summer evening
together, there's extended zoo hours for 10 consecutive
Tuesdays! Open until 7pm, stay on the grounds till 8!
What an excellent idea!

Seward House

Auburn, NY

A lot of important people have walked the halls at 33 South Street in Auburn, New York. Generals Ulysses S. Grant and George Custer, Presidents John Quincy Adams, Andrew Johnson and William McKinley. Even President Bill Clinton visited the Seward House, and I've been told he loved the books in the library so much, he wouldn't leave! Now, you get to walk the halls too!

A Getaway to the William Seward House is a wonderful experience because there is so much important history to take in, like the fact that Seward was a Governor, a state and U.S. Senator and President Lincoln's Secretary of State. And, that Seward was attacked the same night Lincoln was shot! You'll learn all about it and more! The docents are excellent! They have so much to share at this National Historic Landmark!

"One of the foremost politicians of nineteenth century America"

Seward House Historic Museum

33 South Street
Auburn, NY 13021

Scan for map.
Learn how on page 5.

Info:

(315) 252-1283
www.sewardhouse.org
www.tourcayuga.com
Open Tues-Sat 10am-5pm
June - Labor Day open Sunday 1pm-5pm
Closed Mondays and major holidays
Handicapped accessible, please call ahead
Tours start on the hour. Call ahead to be sure of tour availability.
Adults $8, AAA/Seniors/Military $7, Students $5
Children under 6 Free.

Travel Tip:

Visit the Seward House around the holidays! It'll be decorated the same way the Seward Family decorated it back in the mid-1800's! It's absolutely beautiful!

Sky High Aerial Park

Ellicottville, NY

I found an exciting attraction in Western New York that takes you to the tree tops! Sky High Aerial Park requires some guts. This is one of the largest aerial adventure parks of its kind in North America! You'll find this Getaway at Holiday Valley Ski Resort in Ellicottville, New York, Cattaraugus County.

As you enter this 4-acre, wooded spectacle, you'll begin to see zip lines, cables and platforms hidden in the trees. Each of the 9 courses vary in difficulty and are color coded from yellow to black. Only the very brave attempt the double black Commando Course. Never fear, a harness with locking lanyard keeps you safe. Even if you have a fear of heights, you may end up surprising yourself. I personally stopped shaking after the first 10 minutes!

Be sure to wear your hiking clothes and good athletic shoes. Reservations are suggested and children must be at least 7 years old!

If you love zip lines, you may want to try the newly added zip-to-the-bottom Grand Rapids I and II. You'll go from the park to the base via 6 zip lines!

Sky High Aerial Adventure Park

6557 Holiday Valley Road - Route 219
Ellicottville, NY 14731

Scan for map.
Learn how on page 5.

Info:
(716) 699-HIGH (4444)
www.holidayvalley.com/skyhigh
$47 per person for 3 hour sessions
Open every day of the week during
the summer months 9am-6pm.
Open weekends in the spring and fall until the end of November
Be sure to check website for exact times and schedule
This is a 'weather permitting' Getaway!

Travel Tip:
Make time for the Sky High Mountain Coaster! Zigzag down
the mountain along a spiraling metal track in a car that you
control! Open all year...even in winter!

Sonnenberg Gardens

Canandaigua, NY

Who doesn't like walking through a mansion? A Getaway to Sonnenberg Gardens and Mansion State Historic Park in Canandaigua is a trip back in time! This Getaway takes you back to 1887, when New York City bank financier Frederick Ferris Thompson and his wife, Mary Clark, strolled the halls of their 40-room Queen Anne-style home up on the hill.

Today, you can do the same! Once inside, you'll get a view of many of the mansion's stately rooms, like the impressive Great Hall, the Billiard and Trophy Rooms, the Library, Drawing Room, Dining Room, and upstairs, the Master Bedroom! You can't spend the night, but you can spend a few hours in the mansion and on the lush grounds, with 9 amazingly beautiful formal gardens!

So many special events, too! Everything from the annual Father's Day Car & Motorcycle Cruise to Arts at the Gardens!

The mansion is handicap-accessible throughout the first floor. No pets allowed, except handicap service animals.

Sonnenberg Gardens

151 Charlotte St.
Canandaigua, NY 14424

Info:

(585) 394-4922
www.sonnenberg.org
Hours: Open Daily May-October.
Guided Walking Tours Memorial Day
until End of September. Weather
dependent! See website for tour times.
Entrance into the gardens and mansion - $12 Adults, $10 Seniors (60+) and
AAA Members, $6 Students (13-17) and Military w/ ID, $1 Children (4-12)
3 and under free. Guided walking tours included with admission.

Travel Tip:

Be sure to see the Finger Lakes Wine Center in the historic
Bay House near the conservatory. Daily wine tastings! Open
11am to 4pm. Garden admission is not required!

Scan for map.
Learn how on page 5.

Train Ride

Saratoga Springs, NY

One great way to see the colors of fall is to hop aboard a train! But this Train Ride Getaway is very unique. The Saratoga & North Creek Railway has vintage coach cars, and my favorite, dome car seating. Large wrap-around windows up top, so you get the best view of the Adirondack region!

Coach service is comfortable and a good choice for families. My advice is to try out the dome cars if you can...it's so fun! There's white tablecloth service for breakfast or lunch with good food prepared out of the small kitchen down below. The seven stops along the way give you the chance to explore the friendly towns along the First Wilderness Heritage Corridor.

Even though Fall is a good time to go, the train ride is just as enjoyable in the Spring, Summer and Winter! In fact, the seasonal Snow Train brings skiers to Gore Mountain! Schedules have various departure and arrival times depending on the day you choose. Be sure to check their website.

Saratoga & North Creek Railway

26 Station Lane
Saratoga Springs, NY 12866

Scan for map.
Learn how on page 5.

Info:

(877) 726-7245
www.sncrr.com
Adults $30 Coach
$55 for Dome Car
Children $24 Coach, $44
Dome Car. See website for specific
times and fares. Food service is additional.

Travel Tip:

If you're starting your train ride out of Saratoga Springs, take the extra time to enjoy their charming downtown. Great history, the race track, the state park and good restaurants. I recommend Hattie's, 45 Phila Street, for the best fried chicken!

Tree House

It stands 6 stories tall and lurks in the woods! It blends in with the trees so well, you may be looking at it and not even know it! Not to worry! This safe, family Getaway in Thompkins County is a giant Tree House soaring high among the branches at the Cayuga Nature Center.

As you enter this amazing structure, you'll climb a never-ending series of wooden steps and platforms that take you to the top! Some people come to contemplate, others come to climb! It's a great workout!

Scenic Route 89 along Cayuga Lake's west side is where you'll find this fun day trip destination, just a few miles north of Ithaca. On your walk to the tree house, you'll see live animal and nature exhibits. If you like to hike, you can take in the 5 miles of scenic trails of over 120 acres of natural gorges and native wildlife.

There's even a Summer Butterfly Garden! This is a total nature Getaway!

Cayuga Nature Center
1420 Taughannock Blvd (Rt 89)
Ithaca, NY 14850

Scan for map.
Learn how on page 5.

Info:
(607) 273-6260
www.cayuganaturecenter.org
Open Year Round
Memorial Day thru Labor Day: 9am-5pm
Labor Day thru Memorial Day:10am-4pm
Closed Mondays, Thanksgiving, Christmas and New Years
Adults $3, Seniors and Students $2, Children (4-17) $1

Travel Tip:
As you might imagine, the fall season is the best time
to visit when the leaves are full of color!

Waterfall Getaways

O ne thing in New York State that we thankfully have a lot of...waterfalls! They're fun to see and even better when they're free! Here are a few of my absolute faves!

Shhhh! **Grimes Glen Falls** is a hidden gem in Naples, New York and can be found at the very end of Vine Street in the village. There's a place to park and picnic tables, too. Please be respectful of the private properties nearby. You can walk the trail alongside the falls, but the path does end and you may eventually have to walk through the creek to continue. There are 3 main waterfalls, all around 60 feet high! The first 2 waterfalls are easily seen, but it's a strenuous, and possibly dangerous hike to see the third. Consider this Getaway adventurous!

Ithaca Falls is a very peaceful place to get away from it all, yet only a short walk from Route 34, Lake Street in the city. The 75-foot falls cascade over a sloping rock formation creating a continuous, mesmerizing sound. Sometimes you'll find a very relaxed atmosphere, with only local college students taking in the sights. It's not guaranteed, but free parking can occasionally be found in the lot across the street.

Havana Glen Park in Montour Falls, Schuyler County, just south of Watkins Glen on Route 14, has a beautiful, short walking trail. You'll pass some smaller waterfalls and limestone cliffs along McClure Creek, eventually leading to the 41 foot **Eagle Cliff Falls**. A natural swimming hole for many on a hot summer day! At one point, there are steps to climb and the trail can be narrow and slippery, so be careful! The park also has picnic facilities and BBQ grills, plus a playground for kids. Parking fee is $2.

Grimes Glen Falls

Eagle Cliff Falls

Waterfall Getaways

Eagle Cliff Falls in Montour Falls, NY
Grimes Glen Falls in Naples, NY
Ithaca Falls in Ithaca, NY

Info:

www.gowaterfalling.com
These waterfalls are not
handicap accessible.
Waterfalls are open to
the public year round.
Havana Glen Park trail
officially opens mid-May.

Ithaca Falls

Travel Tip:

When hiking, I always like to bring plenty of water and
a snack for some energy. Also, there's a fun app for
iPhone and Android devices called *MapMyHike*. The app
uses your phone's GPS to track and log your hikes.
Great for the hiking enthusiast!

Whirlpool Aero Car

Niagara Falls, Canada

This Getaway isn't on the top of everyone's to-do list when visiting Niagara Falls, Canada. Strangely, most people don't even know it's here, so I aim to change that! Hard to believe because it's been on the banks of the Niagara River since 1916!

After crossing the Rainbow Bridge into Canada and getting yourself onto River Road, don't blink! The Whirlpool Aero Car is easy to miss! At first, boarding the open-air antique cable car might be a bit scary, as it puts you directly above the natural phenomenon, the Niagara Whirlpool! But then you realize that this vantage point is like no other in Niagara Falls! The aerial cable car travels safely along 6 sturdy cables between 2 different points during the 10-minute ride, carrying 35 standing passengers. This is breathtaking, classic Niagara Falls fun!

credit: Niagara Parks Commission

credit: Niagara Parks Commission

Whirlpool Aero Car

3850 Niagara Parkway
Niagara Falls, ON, Canada

Info:

(905) 354-5711
www.niagaraparks.com
Free parking available!
$13.50 Adults, $8.80 Children (6-12)
5 and under free.
Open daily from April-October
weather permitting
This ride is NOT wheelchair accessible

Scan for map.
Learn how on page 5.

Travel Tip:

Head north on River Road to the Butterfly Conservatory, or south to White Water Walk! You are close to both!

White Water Walk

Niagara Falls, Canada

How about a walk on the very wild side? You can do it in Niagara Falls, Canada, at the popular White Water Walk! Even though it's been around since the 1930's, it is still one of those Getaways that many people don't even know about!

The adventure begins with an elevator ride down 230 feet, to the edge of the mighty Niagara River. A well-constructed boardwalk allows you to stroll along at your own pace right next to the river, with two opportunities to descend stairs to take you even closer to the raging river!

The boardwalk is flat, partly shaded and wheelchair accessible. Bring a camera for some amazing shots! You really don't know how 'mighty' the Niagara River is until you're *this* close! A Niagara Falls classic that's very romantic, too!

Simply cross the Rainbow Bridge into Niagara Falls, Canada and follow River Road north. White Water Walk is on your right side. Remember...when traveling into Canada, you must have a current passport or enhanced driver's license. For children 15 and under, an original or copy of birth certificate will suffice.

credit: Niagara Parks Commission

credit: Niagara Parks Commission

White Water Walk
Niagara Pkwy
Niagara Falls, ON L0S 1J0, Canada

**Scan for map.
Learn how on page 5.**

Info:
(905) 374-1221
www.niagaraparks.com
Admission: $10.95 Adults
$7 Children (6-12)
Children 5 and under are free!
Open seasonally, April-October
Handicap Accessible (partial access)

Travel Tip:
Save $$$! Free Parking across the street, *and* kids aged 5 and under are free! In fact, they're free on most of Canada's Niagara Falls attractions!

Willard Memorial Chapel

Even some of the locals don't know about this gem, right in their own back yard! That's what makes Willard Memorial Chapel such a great find! This rare Getaway on Nelson Street in downtown Auburn, NY takes you back more than 115 years, to a chapel whose interior was designed and hand crafted entirely by Louis C. Tiffany and Tiffany Glass and Decorating Company of New York City.

Willard Memorial Chapel is the only complete and unaltered Tiffany-designed religion interior known to exist in the world! And you get to go inside! The stained glass windows, the mosaic floors, the furnishings of oak with inlaid metal and glass mosaic, the amazing church pipe organ and a ton of great local history make this Getaway a true treasure of the Finger Lakes. Ask your tour guide for a peek inside the secret door to the back of the organ!

Willard Memorial Chapel
17 Nelson St.
Auburn, NY 13021

Info:
(315) 252-0339
www.willardchapel.org
www.tourcayuga.com
$4 Suggested donation per person
Regular Hours:
Tuesday-Friday 10am-4pm
January & February:Thursday and Friday 10am-4pm
July & August: Tuesday-Friday 10am-4pm/Sunday 1pm-4pm
Tours are given on the hour, every hour.
Last tour begins at 3pm.

Scan for map.
Learn how on page 5.

Travel Tip:
Each December, you can take in all of Auburn's historic
sites FREE during the annual Open House. So, in addition
to Willard Memorial Chapel, you'll get to tour The Harriet
Tubman Home and the William Seward House...free!
Make a day of it!

SPECIAL HAUNTED SECTION!

Beardslee Castle

Little Falls, NY

HAUNTED

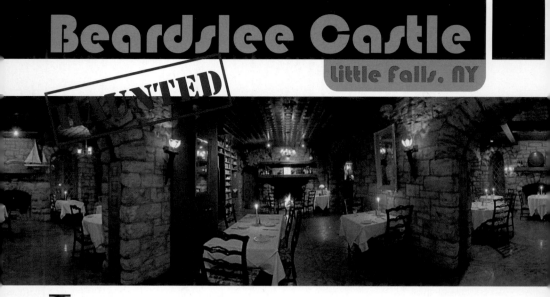

I must admit, I was pretty scared on my first visit to Beardslee Castle...it was the dead of night. I was there to film a show, not about the great American cuisine that people come from all around to enjoy, but to shoot a story on ghosts!

The historic Beardslee Castle is found in Little Falls, NY, between Syracuse and Albany. The castle sits on 8 acres of beautiful grounds and has been a popular restaurant since the 1940's. From seared salmon to grilled duckling, the menu is extensive and it's all delicious! The main floor of the castle is divided into 5 intimate rooms separated by wide stone arch-ways. The original oak floors and ceilings have been beautifully restored. This all adds to a very unique dining experience!

The story goes....In the early 50's, travelers along Route 5 reported seeing a blue light rushing out at their cars and chasing them down the road! Some say the ghost of Mr. Beardslee walks the grounds at night, holding a lantern with a blue light!

Today, owner and Executive Chef Randall Brown, knowledgeable in the castle's history and recent unexplained incidences, seems more than happy to talk about it.....with a devilish grin!

Beardslee Castle

123 Old State Road
Little Falls, NY 13365

**Scan for map.
Learn how on page 5.**

Info:
(315) 823-3000
www.beardsleecastle.com
Entrees $19-$26
Attire is dressy casual or better
Dinner Hours: Thursday, Friday and Saturday: 5pm-9pm
Sunday: 4pm-8pm
Call for reservations

Travel Tip:
Stay too long at the Dungeon bar? Sleep at one of the many nearby bed & breakfasts and inns. Visit the Beardslee website and click on *nearby accommodations* for a list.

Edward Harris House
Rochester, NY

HAUNTED

If you're looking for a Rochester Bed & Breakfast with a little ghostly fun, try the historic Edward Harris House at 35 Argyle Street. This elegant and very comfortable accommodation has antique furnishings, ultra plush bedding, a wonderful breakfast each morning in the formal dining room and continuous coffee, tea and cookies! And yes, according to many, there are a few friendly spirits roaming the halls and rooms!

Out of all of the guest rooms and suites, Rosemary's Suite seems to be the most active when it comes to mysterious mischief...TV turning on by itself, light-switch malfunctions, stereo blasting and no one there! Local mediums and psychics have picked up a lot of spirit activity when entering this room. In fact, they have sensed spirits throughout the entire B&B!

Innkeeper Susan Alvares takes it all in stride and with a sense of humor. She reports that many people call to reserve a room for the night for just that reason alone!

Stay the night with some friendly spirits!

all Edrward Harris house photo credits:
Jumping Rock Photography

Edward Harris House

35 Argyle Street
Rochester, NY 14607

Scan for map.
Learn how on page 5.

Info:
(585) 473-9752 or 1-800-419-1213
www.edwardharrishouse.com
Inn Rates: $169-$225 plus taxes
Rates include breakfast
Smoking permitted on porches and patio areas only.
River Cottage: $200-$225 per night- 3 night minimum
Open year round. No pets.

Travel Tip:
Also available at edwardharrishouse.com, The River Cottage!
A beautifully restored, vintage 1940's Fireman's Cottage, nestled
on the banks of the Genesee River in Scottsville, NY. Plenty of room
for families, or a good Getaway for just the 2 of you. The wood-
burning stone fireplace makes it very romantic!

George Eastman House

3rd from left is Miss Molly

That beautiful Colonial Revival mansion in Rochester on East Avenue sure gets a lot of attention! It should! That's where the father of modern photography and motion picture film used to live! The George Eastman House is a landmark destination to visitors from all over the world and makes for a wonderful Getaway any time of year.

The founder of Eastman Kodak Company lived here from 1905 to 1932 and today, it's yours to explore! 37 rooms, 13 baths and 9 fireplaces! But, it seems to hold a bit more than most may think. Shhhh! A few of the employees have had some unexplained experiences that would lead you to believe that something is lurking up on the 3rd floor. Could it be Mr. Eastman's housekeeper, Miss Molly? A security guard reportedly described seeing a woman just like her, white hair and all, walking the halls late at night! From mysterious footsteps down the back stairway to doors that shutter in the former servants quarters, the George Eastman House may hold more than just great history. Maybe that's why there are no tours at night!

George Eastman House

900 East Avenue
Rochester, NY 14607

**Scan for map.
Learn how on page 5.**

Info:

(585) 271-3361
www.eastmanhouse.org
Adults $12, Seniors (65+) $10, Students $5
Children 12 and under free!
Open Tuesday-Saturday, 10am-5pm, Sunday 11am-5pm
Closed Mondays
Gardens open May-September

Travel Tip:

Mr. Eastman loved his gardens, and you will too! The West
Garden and Rock Garden are accessible without Museum
admission. The Terrace Garden, Library Garden, and East
Vista are accessible with Museum admission.

Miles Wine Cellars

HAUNTED

Himrod, NY

As you drive down Randall Crossing, the winding road just off of Route 14, south of Geneva, New York, a beautiful, white Greek Revival Home comes into view. It's almost as if you've been transported back in time. You have discovered a very popular Finger Lakes winery...and maybe even more!

Miles Wine Cellars, on the shore of Seneca Lake in Himrod, has wine and beer tasting rooms and a seasonal café that serves homemade soups, salads and baked goods. Plus, the cheese is locally made! Miles is one of the only wineries in the country that you can visit by boat complete with a dock tasting room!

What else makes this Getaway unique? It's haunted! Ask the owner, Doug, or the manager, Suzy about the ghostly visitors witnessed on the porch!

In fact, 'Ghost' is the name of their most popular wine, a blend of Chardonnay and Cayuga wines. The story behind the name is just as much fun!

Miles Wine Cellars & Inn

168 Randall Rd.
Himrod, NY 14842

Info:

(607) 243-7742
www.mileswinecellars.com
Tasting Fee $3
Room Rates begin at $150 per night / Double Occupancy
Includes continental breakfast
Open Year Round
Hours: Mon-Sat. 10am-5pm, Sunday 12pm-5pm

Scan for map.
Learn how on page 5.

Travel Tip:

New to the winery...The Inn! There are 2 luxurious guest rooms now available! Choose from the spacious William Miles Suite or the intimate Drake's Landing, both overlooking Seneca Lake.

European Elegance • Stunning Atmosphere • Exquisite Dining • World Class Hospitality

Geneva On The Lake

*Romantic beauty, stunning surroundings, and gourmet cuisine
at a historic hotel where you'll be treated like royalty.*

"One of the 10 most romantic inns in the United States"

- American Historic Inns

Reservations
1-800-3-GENEVA
www.genevaonthelake.com

**GENEVA
ON THE LAKE**
WINE COUNTRY VILLA
& RESORT

1001 Lochland Rd., Route 14, Geneva, NY 14456

Enjoying the book?
Get one for a friend at
TheGetawayGuy.com

Makes a great gift for friends, family and co-workers!

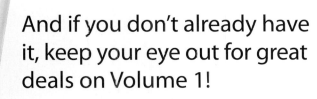

And if you don't already have it, keep your eye out for great deals on Volume 1!

25. Luggage Label

Instead of the that ugly red piece of yarn tied to the handle of your luggage, try slapping on a bright piece of duct tape to the bottom of your suitcase! Luggage usually comes down the chute wheels first. This way, you'll be able to spot yours right away!

24. Get Insured!

Whoops! After just recently jumping into the ocean with my cell phone in my bathing suit pocket, I know the importance of cell phone insurance. Also, travel insurance is a very smart idea, in case of medical issues or trip cancellation. Policies differ so be sure to shop around!

23. Heavy Traffic

I didn't know our seats were next to the bathroom! Don't make this mistake when choosing your seat assignment online for your next flight! First, go to www.SeatGuru.com. You will find every airline and each of their plane's seating chart, showing you which seats on your flight are good ones and which seats to avoid!

22. Time Your Ticket

Don't you hate it when the fare on the airline ticket you just bought goes DOWN? Check out this website; www.Bing.com/Travel. It has a Farecast feature that tries to predict price changes. I find it to be quite helpful.

21. Get Lucky

Sometimes a late check-in can result in an upgrade at the hotel. The chances of an upgrade increase even more if you're staying just one night. Rooms are not likely to be sold later in the day anyway, so you might just get lucky!

20. Table Tactic

Can't get a reservation at the best restaurant in town? Try this technique that works most of the time; use the concierge at your hotel to make that reservation. They have a lot of pull. Or, if your hotel doesn't have this service, contact the concierge at the big hotel across the street! It works!

19. Wipe Out

Bring your Lysol Wipes to wipe down these four very important items in your hotel room!

1. TV Remote
2. Telephone
3. Toilet Flusher and Seat
4. Door Knob

18. When to Book

According to Travel & Leisure, the best time to book a hotel room for the best rate is one week before your trip. Booking months before really does not give you the best rate in most cases. T&L's research shows that your best rate, on average, is one week out. For an even better rate...pay in advance! Ask!

17. When in Rome

While walking the beautiful streets of Rome, Italy, you only have to buy water once! I use my water bottle everywhere I go, refilling it at Rome's many free-running water stations. They're everywhere, with cold, clean, fresh water from the mountains! Hard to believe, but true!!

16. Rental Rate Relief

Looking for the best car rental price? Check out the new online consolidator www.autoslash.com! It searches out discounts, applies them to your rental when you book and automatically rebooks you at the lower rate if the price drops!

5. Carry-on Crunch

With so many travelers trying to escape the 'checked-bag fees', everyone now has an extra carry-on. As a result, no overhead space anymore! Good chance you'll be forced to stick your carry-on under the seat in front of you which leaves you no foot room. Try purchasing a 'choice-seat' when choosing your seat assignment online. The fee is less than the 'checked-bag' charge and it bumps you up to an early boarding zone, which gives you plenty of time and space to stow your carry-on bags.

14. Laptop Mix-up

One of the biggest problems at airport security these days is laptops getting mixed up. To avoid picking up the wrong one, simply tape your business card to the bottom of your laptop.

3. Damage Control

On a recent Getaway, I noted front bumper scratches on my rental car. A rental representative assured me it was OK. I insisted she still document the damage on my contract before I accepted the car. Good thing! On my rental return, the damage was seen and, without the written documentation, I was about to be charged! Here's the deal, at bigger airports, you simply get your keys and are told where the car is located in the lot. There is usually no one around! My advice is to inspect the car yourself before you leave and, if you see any damage, get someone from the rental company to write it down.

12. Reviews That Reveal

When trying to choose the right hotel or resort, I always go to www.TripAdvisor.com. Its reviews come from real people who were just customers; honest comments that give you a clear picture of where you're about to spend your money. They also list the most popular properties with *People's #1 Choice*. A very revealing website!

11. More Choice = Lower Price

When searching for the best deal on airfare, try a web site that gives you ALL the airline choices, like www.Kayak.com. It makes the search for the best fares and schedules much easier!

10. Free Upgrades

I like to use this one..."This is a very special trip for us."
A very good line to use at the front desk when checking
into a hotel. Say it with a smile and politely inquire about
a room upgrade. More times than not, you'll score!

9. Stranded!

Bringing your passport on your next Getaway? Before you
leave, be sure to make 2 copies of your identification page.
Keep 1 copy with you in a separate part of your luggage.
Leave the other copy with a friend or family member. This
way, if your passport is lost or stolen, you have a back-up
that can be sent to you in an emergency.

8. Head of the Class

From time to time, cruise lines will offer special discounts
on select sailings to customers who are teachers! Qualifying
teachers must present a photocopy of their teacher's certification,
union card or a letter from their principal on school letterhead. So,
if you're a teacher and going on a cruise, do your homework
and check around!

7. Traveling with Kids?

Bathroom stops can sometimes be a challenge. Gas station,
fast food and rest stop restrooms can sometimes be a little
scary, so look for a chain motel! Just off highway exits,
they are usually right in the lobby and much cleaner!

6. Dear Robbers,

Just to be safe, on your next fly-away Getaway, don't put
your home address on your luggage tags! You don't need
to let everyone know where your empty home is located!
Use a business card in your luggage tag, and put one inside
your luggage too!

5. Socially Smart

Many criminals are now targeting homes when they know you're traveling. They use social media outlets like Facebook to see where and when you are tagged in photos. Remember that the digital content you share can often travel much farther than the close friends you intended it for. Be sure to use the website's filters to limit who can see your posts.

4. Picnic = Quiet Travel

Pack a picnic when traveling with the kids on your next road trip this summer! Not only will you save money, but kids tend to use up more energy at a picnic site along the way. This means they may nap a bit when you get back in the car!

3. Woof and the Roof

Nearly 30 million Americans travel with their pets every year, but pet-friendly hotels are sometimes hard to find. Here's a travel tip with bite...try Motel 6, Best Western or Red Roof Inn. They all have chain-wide policies to accept pets! Individual properties do, however, have their own discretion on how policies are applied on an individual basis, so call ahead!

2. Got the Flying Blues?

Flying anytime soon? Go mid-week! You can expect shorter lines and better air fares on Tuesdays and Wednesdays for domestic and international travel.

1. What a View!

On your next Getaway, if you want to find a hotel room that doesn't overlook the parking lot, try the website www.RoomsWithGreatViews.com. Travelers have submitted great photos of views from their room, giving you all the information you need, including the room number!

Travel Notes

I always love to hear other people's travel stories! Feel free to email me the tales of your Getaway adventures at

mike@thegetawayguy.com

Maybe your story will end up on TheGetawayGuy.com!

_____

_____

_____

_____

_____

_____

_____

_____

_____

_____

_____

_____

_____

_____

_____

_____

_____

Travel Notes

I always love to hear other people's travel stories! Feel free to email me the tales of your Getaway adventures at

mike@thegetawayguy.com

Maybe your story will end up on TheGetawayGuy.com!

_____

_____

_____

_____

_____

_____

_____

_____

_____

_____

_____

_____

_____

_____

_____

_____

_____

_____

Travel Notes

I always love to hear other people's travel stories! Feel free to email me the tales of your Getaway adventures at

mike@thegetawayguy.com

Maybe your story will end up on TheGetawayGuy.com!